Salt Dough Fun

I Made It Myself!

Brigitte Casagranda

GARETH**STEVENS**

GS PUBLISHING

A Member of the WRC Media Family of Companies

To Marie, Sophie, and Baptiste

The author and publishers thank Céline for the photographs.

All designs in this book are the exclusive creations of Brigitte Casagranda.
They may not be reproduced for exhibit or sale purposes of any kind or in any form.

Please visit our web site at: www.garethstevens.com
For a free color catalog describing Gareth Stevens Publishing's
list of high-quality books and multimedia programs, call
1-800-542-2595 (USA) or 1-800-387-3178 (Canada).
Gareth Stevens Publishing's fax: (414) 332-3567.

Library of Congress Cataloging-in-Publication Data

Casagranda, Brigitte.
   [Drôle de boules. English]
   Salt dough fun / Brigitte Casagranda.
      p. cm. — (I made it myself!)
   ISBN 0-8368-5967-7 (lib. bdg.)
   1. Salt dough craft—Juvenile literature.
 I. Title. II. Series.
 TT880.C343613 2005
 745.5—dc22   2005046499

This edition first published in 2006 by
Gareth Stevens Publishing
A Member of the WRC Media Family of Companies
330 West Olive Street, Suite 100
Milwaukee, Wisconsin 53212 USA

This U.S. edition copyright © 2006 by Gareth Stevens, Inc.
Original edition first published by Larousse-Bordas, Paris,
France, under the title *Tout en pâte à sel: Drôles de Boules*,
copyright © Dessain et Tolra / Larousse, Paris 2004.

Photography: Cactus Studio
Translation: Muriel Castille
English text: Dorothy L. Gibbs
Gareth Stevens series editor: Dorothy L. Gibbs
Gareth Stevens art direction and cover design: Tammy West
Gareth Stevens graphic design: Jenni Gaylord

Printed in the United States of America

1 2 3 4 5 6 7 8 9 09 08 07 06 05

CONTENTS

Recipe for Salt Dough

The salt dough figures in this book have to be baked in a hot oven to make the dough harden. The instructions for each project show the amount of baking time needed and the temperature of the oven. Keep in mind that these times and temperatures are only approximate and may vary considerably from one oven to another.

Caution!

ALWAYS ASK A GROWN-UP TO TURN THE OVEN ON AND OFF FOR YOU AND, WHEN YOUR WORK IS READY FOR BAKING, ALWAYS HAVE A GROWN-UP PUT IT INTO OR TAKE IT OUT OF THE OVEN. DO NOT TOUCH THE BAKED DOUGH UNTIL IT HAS HAD TIME TO COOL COMPLETELY.

Materials:
- flour
- salt
- medium-size drinking glass
- medium-size mixing bowl
- wooden spoon
- water

Pour 2 glasses of flour and 1 glass of salt into the mixing bowl and stir them together with a wooden spoon. Add water, a little at a time, and stir some more. Add just enough water to make the dough thick but not sticky.

Place the dough on a table and knead it until it is soft and smooth, with no lumps. You knead dough by pushing on it and squeezing it with your hands. If the dough is too sticky or too soft, add a little more flour. If the dough is hard and crumbly, add a little more water. Then knead the dough some more.

To start making your figures, take just enough dough for one project. The rest of the dough can be saved for a few hours in a plastic bag with a zip top or a plastic container with a tight-fitting lid. If the dough gets too soft, you just have to add some flour and knead it again.

You can make your figures right on a baking sheet, or when you're done making a figure, you can place it on a piece of aluminum foil. Halfway through baking, remove your figures from the baking sheet or the foil and place them directly on the oven rack (see CAUTION! on page 4).

5

Little Lion

This little lion is not dangerous! It is a fun figure to play with or to use as a decoration. After baking it and letting it cool, paint your lion yellow, like this lion, or some other bright color, then paint a face on it. Don't forget the whiskers!

Materials:
- salt dough
- dull knife
- paintbrush
- water

Baking time:
40 to 60 minutes

Oven temperature:
225° Fahrenheit
(100° Celsius)

1

Make balls of salt dough:
- 1 large ball for the lion's body
- 1 medium ball for the head
- 4 small balls for the paws
- 12 to 16 little balls for the mane
- 1 tiny ball for the nose

Roll a small amount of salt dough into a rope for the tail. Cut tiny slits into one end of the rope to make a tuft. Flatten 2 little balls of dough into small circles to make the lion's cheeks.

2

Put the large ball of dough (the body) in front of you. Press the balls you made for the lion's paws and head into place on the large ball. Press the plain end of the salt dough rope (the tail) onto the lion's back.

3

Brush some water all over the lion's head. (The water will help the balls for the lion's mane and nose and the circles for its cheeks stick to the lion's head.) Press little balls all around the head to make the lion's mane. Press the tiny ball onto the front of the head to make a nose. Press the two flat circles onto the front of the head, under the nose, for the lion's cheeks.

Woolly Sheep

A curly-haired sheep is an easy farm animal figure to make. Giving your sheep golden-colored wool, like this one, is easy, too. After the sheep bakes for one hour, brush its curls with a little bit of milk and put it back into the oven for about 15 minutes at 250° F (125° C).

Materials:
- salt dough
- dull knife
- plastic drinking straw

Baking time:
  1 hour

Oven temperature:
  225° F (100° C)

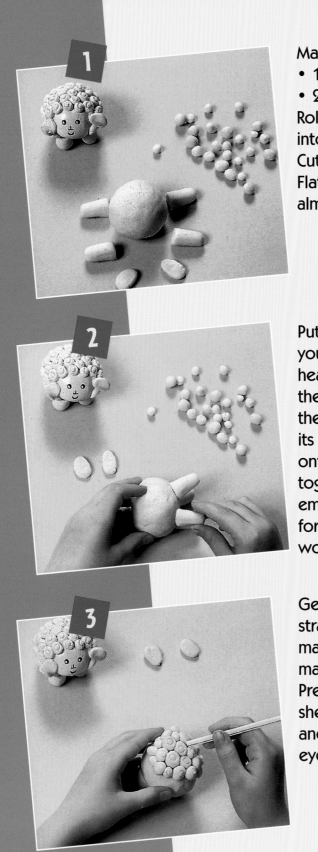

Make balls of salt dough:
• 1 large ball for the body
• 20 or more little balls for the wool
Roll 2 medium balls of salt dough into short logs with rounded ends. Cut each log in half to make 4 legs. Flatten 2 small balls of dough into almond shapes to make ears.

Put the large ball of dough in front of you. This ball is the sheep's body (the head is included in the body). Press the cut end of each leg into place on the body. With the sheep standing on its legs, press all the little balls of dough onto the body. Place these balls tightly together, but don't forget to leave an empty space on the front of the body for the sheep's face. Flatten the balls of wool a little as you press them in place.

Gently push one end of a plastic drinking straw into each little flattened ball to make circles in the dough. The circles make the sheep's wool look curly. Press one ear onto each side of the sheep's head. After baking your sheep and letting it cool, you can paint on its eyes, nose, and mouth.

9

Beep Beep

These cute little cars are great toys for indoor play on a rainy day. And they are so easy to make that you can have lots of them. After baking your cars and letting them cool, paint them each a different color — the brighter, the better!

Materials:
- salt dough
- rolling pin
- large round cookie cutter
- dull knife
- paintbrush
- water

Baking time:
  30 minutes

Oven temperature:
  225° F (100° C)

Use a rolling pin to flatten a very large ball of salt dough. Cut out circles of dough with a round cookie cutter. Cut each circle in half to make two cars.

For each car, make 2 little balls of salt dough (for wheels) and 3 tiny balls (2 for wheel decorations and 1 for a headlight). Cut two spaces into the straight side of each car (one space near each end) to make places for the wheels.

Brush some water over one side of each of the bigger balls of dough. Press these balls into the spaces you cut out for the wheels. Press one of the tiny balls onto the top of each bigger ball to decorate the wheels. Brush some water over the last tiny ball and press that ball onto the front of the car to make a headlight.

Perky Penguin

Most penguins live in ice and snow, but this penguin needs to bake in a hot oven, just like any other salt dough figure. When your penguin has finished baking, take it out of the oven so it can cool off. Then you can paint it and glaze it.

Materials:
- salt dough
- dull knife
- paintbrush
- water

Baking time:
1 hour

Oven temperature:
start at 150° F (60° C) and increase to 225° F (100° C) about halfway through the baking time

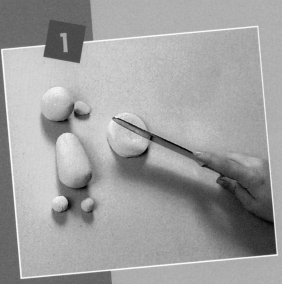

Shape 1 large ball of salt dough into a long oval. (An oval is the shape of an egg.) The oval will be the body of your penguin. Make 2 small balls of dough for the penguin's feet and make 1 tiny ball of dough, pinching one side of it to form a beak. Make 2 medium-sized balls of dough. One will be the penguin's head. Flatten the other one with your hand to form a circle. Cut the circle in half to make wings.

Place all of the salt dough shapes you made in step one in front of you and arrange them to form a penguin.

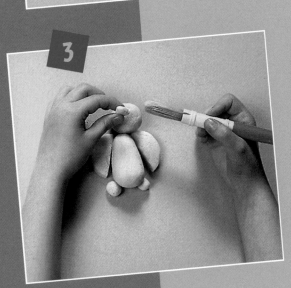

Brush each shape with some water before you press the shapes together to attach them.

13

Dotted Ladybug

Some people say that you can tell the age of a ladybug by counting how many black dots it has on its back. You can decide the age of this salt dough ladybug just by painting that number of black dots on its back.

Materials:
- salt dough
- paintbrush
- water

Baking time:
1 hour

Oven temperature:
225° F (100° C)

Make balls of salt dough:
- 1 large ball for the ladybug's body
- 1 medium ball for the head
- 6 small balls for the legs
- 2 tiny balls for the eyes

Brush some water on one end of the large ball (the body) and press the medium ball (the head) onto that end to attach the head to the body. Brush all of the small balls with water and press them onto the sides of the body, near the bottom. Attach three balls on each side. These balls are the ladybug's legs.

Brush water over both of the tiny balls (the eyes) and press them onto the top of the ladybug's head. After baking your ladybug and letting it cool, you can paint its body red. Let the red paint dry before you use black paint on its legs and head. Then, just add dots!

Big Green Frog

A big frog with big eyes is fun to make — and very easy. Eight balls of salt dough and a few sturdy toothpicks are all it takes. For your big frog to be green and shiny, just add paint and glaze. Now, hop to it!

Materials:
- salt dough
- toothpicks
- paintbrush
- water

Baking time:
1 hour

Oven temperature:
start at 100° F (40° C) and increase to 225° F (100° C) about halfway through the baking time

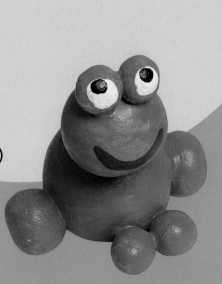

Make balls of salt dough:
- 1 large ball for the frog's body
- 1 medium ball for the head
- 4 small balls for the legs
- 2 small balls for the eyes

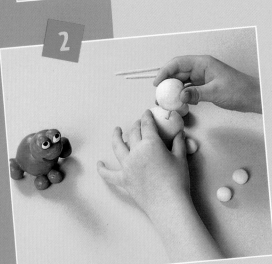

Put the large ball of dough (the body) in front of you. Push a toothpick into the ball until only half of the toothpick is sticking out. Gently push the medium ball (the head) onto the toothpick until the head is touching the body. The toothpick will keep the frog's head up straight.

Brush two small balls with water and press them together. Attach them to the front of the large ball of dough, placing them at the bottom of the ball. These are the frog's front legs. Attach one small ball on each side of the large ball, at the back and near the bottom of the ball. These are the frog's back legs. Press two small balls onto the top of the frog's head for eyes. Be sure to brush water on each ball before attaching it.

17

Colorful Caterpillar

You can make the body of a salt dough caterpillar with either flat circles or round balls — with feet or without feet. Whichever caterpillar design you choose, be sure you make it colorful!

Materials:
- salt dough
- short, thin, wooden sticks
- rolling pin
- large round cookie cutter or jar lid
- small round cookie cutter or jar lid
- paintbrush
- water

Baking time:
1½ hours

Oven temperature:
225° F (100° C)

Make balls of salt dough:
- 1 medium ball for a head
- 3 small balls for antennae and a tail
- 2 little balls for eyes

Gently push each of two small balls onto one end of a thin wooden stick. Use a rolling pin to flatten a very large lump of salt dough. Cut out 6 circles of dough with a large round cookie cutter or jar lid and 6 more circles with a small round cookie cutter or jar lid.

Brush some water over each large circle and press a small circle on top of it. Then attach all of the circles together in a line. Be sure to brush water on the dough to help hold the circles together. Brush some water over one side of the medium ball (the head) and press it onto one end of the line of salt dough circles. Brush some water over one side of the third small ball and press it onto the other end of the line of circles.

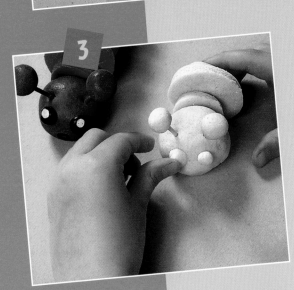

Gently push the wooden sticks with the small balls on them (the antennae) into the top of the caterpillar's head. Be sure to leave some of each stick showing. Press the two little balls (the eyes) onto the front of the head. After baking your caterpillar and letting it cool, paint each section a different bold, bright color.

Bird of Paradise

You can bake this beautiful bird with its feathers on! Even at 225° F (100° C), the feathers won't burn. Paint or glaze, however, might damage the feathers, so after the bird is baked, do not paint or glaze its body. All you need to do to finish your bird is paint two little black eyes on its head and paint its beak yellow.

Materials:
- salt dough
- sturdy wooden toothpicks
- multicolored feathers

Baking time:
40 to 60 minutes

Oven temperature:
start at 150° F (60° C) and increase to 225° F (100° C) about halfway through the baking time

1 Make 1 large salt dough ball for the bird's body and 1 medium ball for its head. Make 1 tiny ball and pinch it between your thumb and index finger to form a beak. Put the large ball of dough (the body) in front of you and push a sturdy wooden toothpick into it, leaving about half of the toothpick sticking out.

2 Push the medium ball of dough (the head) onto the toothpick until the head and body of the bird are touching. Press the bird's beak into place on the front of the bird's head. Brushing a little water on the wide end of the beak will help it stick better to the head.

3 Gently push multicolored feathers into the back and sides of the bird's body to make its tail and wings. Now your bird is ready to bake!

21

Striped Cat

A big striped tomcat, a small gray female, and a mischievous little kitten — what a family! You can paint your cat all one color or give it stripes or spots — or even speckles, if you like. But don't forget to glaze your cat after the paint dries so its colorful coat will shine.

Materials:
- salt dough
- water

Baking time:
  40 to 60 minutes

Oven temperature:
  start at 150° F (60° C)
  and increase to 225° F
  (100° C) about halfway
  through the baking time

Make balls of salt dough:
- 1 large ball for the cat's body
- 1 medium ball for the head
- 4 small balls for the paws
- 4 little balls for the ears and cheeks
- 1 tiny ball for the nose

Flatten two of the little balls with your hand to make cheeks and shape the other two with your fingers to make the cat's ears. Roll a small amount of salt dough into a rope for the cat's tail.

Put the large ball of dough (the body) in front of you. Brush the medium ball (the head) with a little water and press it onto the cat's body. Press the two little flattened pieces of dough onto the front of the cat's head, placing them side by side with the edges touching each other. These are the cat's cheeks. Now, press the tiny ball (the nose) right on top of where the two cheeks meet.

Wait until after you press the cat's paws and tail into place to add the two little ears. Putting the ears on last will help keep you from damaging them. The ears must stay straight up on top of the cat's head.

Final Touches

PAINTING

The best paints to use on salt dough figures are water-based acrylic or poster paints. Primary colors, such as red, blue, yellow, and green, will make your figures look their brightest. Use a thicker brush to paint large surfaces. Use thinner brushes to paint small details. Be sure to clean your brushes often — change the water often, too! Always have a clean rag handy to wipe your washed brushes and to clean up paint splatters.

GLAZING

A glaze is a clear coating that will protect your salt dough figures and give them a shiny finish. It is a lot like the varnish used to protect woodwork. You will need help from a grown-up to glaze your figures. Place them on old newspapers to protect your work area and brush two or three coats of glaze onto each figure. After each coat, you need to wait about 30 minutes for the glaze to dry. You should use an acrylic glaze that is odorless and cleans up with water. Although these glazes are easy to use, you always need to be very careful working with them or even being around them.